QUICK GUIDE TO FINANCIAL SKILLS

QUICK GUIDE TO

LIVING ON A BUDGET

By Jenny Crooks-Johnson

BrightPoint Press

San Diego, CA

BrightPoint Press

an imprint of ReferencePoint Press, Inc.
Printed in the United States

For more information, contact:
BrightPoint Press
PO Box 27779
San Diego, CA 92198
www.BrightPointPress.com

LIBRARY OF CONGRESS CATALOGING-IN-PUBLICATION DATA

Names: Crooks-Johnson, Jenny, author.
Title: Quick guide to living on a budget / by Jenny Crooks-Johnson.
Other titles: Living on a budget
Description: San Diego, CA: BrightPoint Press, [2025] | Series: Quick guide to financial skills | Includes bibliographical references and index. | Audience: Grades 7-9
Identifiers: LCCN 2024004137 (print) | LCCN 2024004138 (eBook) | ISBN 9781678209087 (hardcover) | ISBN 9781678209094 (eBook)
Subjects: LCSH: Budgets, Personal--Juvenile literature. | Financial literacy--Juvenile literature.
Classification: LCC HG179 .C7485 2025 (print) | LCC HG179 (eBook) | DDC 332.024--dc23/eng/20240309
LC record available at https://lccn.loc.gov/2024004137
LC eBook record available at https://lccn.loc.gov/2024004138

CONTENTS

AT A GLANCE

- A budget is a plan for spending and saving money.
- People can use records such as bank and credit card statements to review past spending. They can use this information to create a budget.
- Organizing a budget into categories helps people analyze their spending.
- Fixed expenses are always the same. Examples include rent and car payments. Variable expenses can change from month to month. Examples include groceries and entertainment costs.
- Dividing budget categories into fixed and variable expenses can make it easier to reduce spending.
- If a budget is out of balance, a person needs to increase income or reduce expenses.

- Tracking and reviewing spending are the best ways to stick to a budget plan.
- People can track their spending manually. They can also use apps or spreadsheets.
- Keeping financial goals and values in sight helps people stay motivated to keep to their budgets.
- Waiting before making purchases is a way to control impulse spending.

MARY'S MONEY PROBLEMS

Mary sighs. She hugs her knees to her chest and stares at her phone. The words ***insufficient*** *funds* and ***overdraft fee*** stare back at her. She recently finished a training course. It helped her get a job as a veterinary assistant. She's making more money than she ever has before. So why does she keep running out of it?

Mary looks around. Her one-bedroom apartment is nice. She thought it was

Struggling with debt can feel overwhelming.

In addition to the cost of a car, people should budget for insurance, gas, and repairs.

affordable. But she spends more on rent and utility bills than she had expected.

Priya is a new friend from work. She is about to pick Mary up to go out for dinner. Mary had thought that sounded better than cooking. But now she's worried about the cost. *I guess I'll just have to put it on my credit card*, Mary thinks. She heads outside to Priya's car.

"Thanks for picking me up," Mary says as they drive to the restaurant. "I'll get a car someday if I can ever afford it."

"This car is beat up, but at least I don't have a car payment," Priya says.

"How did you do that? Mary asks.

"My uncle helped me get it from an auction. We fixed it up together. The hard part was saving up the cash."

"I can't even pay all my bills," Mary says. "I don't think I could ever save enough."

"I had that problem too," Priya replies. "But then I got serious and made a budget. I had to make some spending changes to make it work. It took a couple years to save enough."

"I'm scared a budget would just tell me everything I *can't* do," Mary says.

Priya smiles. "Actually, I feel freer now that I have a plan. Even tonight's fun is part of my budget."

They talk about work for a while. But Mary is still thinking about budgets. She would love to feel free like Priya does. "Can you tell me more about how to budget?" she asks.

A budget can help someone living alone for the first time keep track of her money.

"It's really not that hard! I'd be glad to help you," Priya says.

MARY MAKES A BUDGET PLAN

Three days later, they sit down in Mary's apartment. Mary brings out recent bank and credit card **statements**. Priya pulls

Friends can work together to find ways to have fun without spending money.

out highlighters. She helps Mary highlight spending categories in different colors. They create a budget **spreadsheet**.

"The bad news is that your budget doesn't balance right now," Priya says. "You're spending more than you're making. The good news is there are ways to balance it. You need to cut expenses. It would help if you could earn more money, too." She sees Mary's discouraged face. "I know it seems hard, but trust me. It's worth it."

A year later, Mary is saving money by living with a roommate. She canceled her gym membership and Netflix subscription. Now she jogs outside and gets movies from the library. She also suggests cheaper ways to have fun with her friends. And she started a small side business selling homemade crafts online.

Mary reviews the money she spends each week. If she is over in a category, she cuts back. She is still taking the bus to work. But she is also saving money for a car. Her budget even lets her donate to an animal charity every month. Best of all, Mary's budget gives her peace of mind.

People can sell crafts and other products online or at fairs and markets.

CHAPTER ONE

CREATING A BUDGET

A budget is a plan for spending money. Budgets let people know where their money is going. Tracking their money can keep people from spending too much. This helps them avoid harmful debt.

Budgets also help people meet their goals. Most of all, living on a budget creates financial freedom. Money expert Dave Ramsey says, "You must gain control over

Bank and credit card statements show a person's transactions during a specific period, usually a month.

Out
In
Balance
1191.42
1091.41
1022.7
984.55
924.54
903.76
100.01
68.71
38.15
60.01
20.78
256.47
13.98
4539 7885
MONTH/YEAR
VALID FROM
07/12
EXPIRES END

Spreadsheets can make automatic calculations. This makes them especially helpful for creating budgets.

your money, or the lack of it will forever control you."[1]

ON AVERAGE

Many people create monthly budgets. They figure out their average monthly income and expenses. Using records from the past year will help in getting accurate numbers.

Sometimes a person does not have records from a whole year. In this case, a person can use records from as many months as possible. These records include credit card and bank statements. Cash transactions will not show up on a statement. Saving receipts for cash purchases helps people keep track of them. A person could record cash spent in notes on a phone, in a physical notebook, or on an app. One way to record cash earnings is to deposit them in a bank. This makes it easier to track them.

A total yearly amount divided by twelve gives the monthly average. Using average numbers allows for expenses that change throughout the year. For example, a person may spend more money around holidays.

Income can also go up and down. Some people are paid once per week. Months with five weeks will show more income than months with four weeks. Other people have businesses where income changes every month. When making a budget, people should use their **net** income for calculations.

BUDGET CATEGORIES

Assigning expenses to categories makes it easier to analyze spending. Some people use colored highlighters to sort expenses on their financial statements. Other people use apps that automatically put purchases into categories. A person can make changes if the app puts money into the wrong category. People can use the categories that make the most sense for them. No matter what categories people use, they will have fixed and variable expenses.

Fixed expenses mostly stay the same. Some examples include rent or mortgage payments, car payments, tuition, and cell phone bills. Gym memberships, some utilities, and insurance are usually fixed expenses.

Sorting expenses into categories can make it easier to see how a person spends money.

Variable expenses are more flexible. Groceries, entertainment, and clothing are some examples. Transportation, repairs, haircuts, and home decoration can also be variable. These expenses vary from month to month. People usually have more power to change their variable expenses.

Variable expenses can be harder to plan into a budget. Calculating a yearly average can give a good estimate. For example, Mason includes car maintenance and gas in his transportation category. He looks at his records from the past year. He usually spends around $30 a month. But in June he took a road trip. He spent $100 that month. He had a $200 repair in October. When he calculates his budget, he allows $50 per month for transportation. He may not spend that much each month. But leaving room in the budget will help if he has surprise expenses.

CREATE THE BUDGET

Mary wants to create a budget. She can do this by using paper or a computer program. First, Mary calculates her average income

The Cash Envelope Budget Method

Studies show that people spend less money when they use cash instead of a credit or debit card. The cash envelope method takes advantage of this. To use this method, people put cash into envelopes labeled for each of their spending categories. During the month, they use only the cash in each envelope to buy items in that category.

MARY'S MONTHLY BUDGET

Average Monthly Income	
Net vet tech salary (after taxes and insurance)	$3,036
Savings account interest	$5
Net Etsy business income (after expenses)	$100
Total Average Monthly Income	**$3,141**

Fixed Expenses		Variable Expenses	
Renters insurance	$15	Portion of gas/electric & water	$75
Portion of rent	$850	Haircuts	$30
Portion of garbage service	$20	Medical/dental/vision care	$50
Portion of internet	$31	Groceries	$350
Cell phone bill	$144	Clothing	$25
Student loan payment	$250	Gifts	$25
Bus pass	$52	Entertainment	$100
Car savings fund	$100	Miscellaneous	$25
Emergency fund	$50	Credit card interest	$52
Retirement account	$50	Total Average Variable Expenses	$732
Monthly charity donation	$25		
Total Average Fixed Expenses	$1,587		
Total Variable + Fixed Expenses			$2,319
Average income - Average expenses =			$822 left over

Mary can use the leftover money in her budget to pay off extra debt or build a savings fund.

and expenses. She includes all income sources, such as paychecks or bank interest. Then Mary adds them up to get a total monthly income. Now she writes her average income at the top of the sheet.

Next, Mary lists the averages for each fixed expense category. These are followed by the averages for variable expenses. This makes it easier to see where her money is going. Finally, Mary adds up all her expenses. She subtracts the total expenses from her income. If the number is positive, she has money left over. But if the number is negative, she needs to start balancing her budget.

CHAPTER TWO

BALANCING A BUDGET

People should try not to spend more money than they earn. An unbalanced budget has more expenses than income. People can balance their budgets by reducing spending or making more money.

Reducing spending is an important way to balance a budget. People have the most day-to-day control over variable spending. Small expenses add up. Someone might buy a $5 cup of coffee each day. This adds

To save money when grocery shopping, people can plan their meals based on what the store has on sale. Eating at home is usually less expensive than eating out.

up to $150 a month. There are steps people can take to cut down on daily expenses. They can plan meals for the week. Cooking at home and eating leftovers can cut costs. People can look for sales on items they use a lot. They can also learn how to do their own simple home and car repairs. Many online videos teach these basics.

Living on a budget does not mean people cannot have fun. Low-cost entertainment includes nature walks, potlucks, and free public events. People can also use their local libraries to check out movies, books, and music.

Miriam Johnson is a college student. She says, "I don't have a lot of money for entertainment, so me and my friends find cheap ways to have fun. We do game

Living with other people is one way to lower housing costs.

nights and go on walks. We also find free food around campus or make a roommate dinner together instead of going out."[2]

CUTTING FIXED EXPENSES

Fixed expenses are often the largest part of people's budgets. Finding ways to cut costs on these expenses can be more difficult than variable expenses. To lower housing costs, people might consider living with roommates. Sometimes landlords offer reduced rent to tenants who make repairs, mow the lawn, or shovel snow. Good tenants might be able to negotiate lower rent at lease renewal. Landlords may prefer to keep a good tenant around instead of risking having an empty property or a bad tenant.

Some landlords might lower rent for tenants who are willing to shovel snow.

There are other ways to reduce fixed expenses. People can shop around for cheaper insurance or phone plans. People can also cancel gym memberships, paid apps, or online subscriptions they don't use. They can look into refinancing or payment plans for loans. These often result in lower payments.

Sometimes people can reduce utility bills. Saving energy can help people save money. People can adjust the thermostat to less extreme temperatures. A smart thermostat can change the temperature automatically when people aren't home. People can

Smart thermostats can adjust the temperature at certain times or when people leave the house. This saves energy, which saves money on utility bills.

insulate their water heaters. They can also turn down the heater's temperature. Taking shorter showers saves on heat and water.

Some energy companies or state organizations offer programs to save energy. Some companies offer energy inspections. Workers come to a home. They try to find ways people can save energy. They look for appliances that use more energy than they should. They check windows and doors for gaps. Filling gaps helps keep outside air from getting in. Some programs offer free or reduced-price smart thermostats to help people save energy.

MAKING MORE MONEY

Increasing income is usually more difficult than cutting expenses. But it can be done.

One way is through work. Some people seek training to get a higher-paying job. People might also take on an additional job. This could be formal work, such as food service or retail. People can also do small jobs for friends and family. This could be babysitting, yard work, or pet care.

The 50/30/20 Budget

Senator Elizabeth Warren helped create the 50/30/20 budget. Her plan suggests 50 percent of net income goes to basic needs. Then 30 percent can be spent on wants. The final 20 percent is for savings. These savings can be used to pay down debt. They can also be put into emergency funds, retirement accounts, and other savings goals. Reducing needed expenses to half of income can lead to financial independence.

Another option is to increase passive income. This is income that people earn when they are not actively working. *Passive* does not mean *easy*. Some forms of passive income require money and work up front. They may take a long time to start making a profit. But they can be a good way to earn extra income over time.

There are many ways to earn passive income. A successful blogger might sell ad space on her website. A photographer might sell his photos online. Money in a savings account earns interest with no extra effort. William Johnson is a college student. He and his friends designed shirts in high school. They found a website that would print a shirt each time one was ordered. William and his friends started selling shirts.

People with a strong online following can sell ads for passive income.

They made a website and TikTok videos to advertise. They worked hard to set up. And it did take some time to maintain. But once the business was set up, they made sales even when they were not working. Then they split the profits. William says, "The passive income we got from our business helped us focus on high school while also being able to save money for college."[3]

Balancing a budget takes effort. But having a balanced budget helps people stay free of debt. It helps them meet their goals. It is a financially sustainable way to live.

CHAPTER THREE

STICKING TO A BUDGET

Modern life is busy. Advertising is everywhere. It is easy to let spending get out of control. These factors can make it hard to stick to budget goals.

To keep a budget on the right path, people should track and review their spending. This takes time to learn. But practicing for several months can create a routine. If a person regularly makes time to

Budgeting apps help people keep track of their spending.

Tracking spending helps a person know if he is sticking to his budget.

track and review spending, the tasks will become easier.

TRACKING SPENDING

Budget apps are one way to track spending. These apps can pull account information from a person's bank and credit cards. They divide the spending into categories. Then they update the total money spent in each category. Most apps allow a person to adjust categories to match their needs. Apps can also send notices when a category is over the budget limits.

People can also track expenses manually. They can use a notebook. They can use note apps or spreadsheets on a phone or computer. They can even track their budget on a piece of paper in their wallet. They record their spending and subtract it from the budget amount. Then they can easily see how much is left.

Budgets might feel overwhelming. Focusing on two or three spending categories can help. Megan McCallson is a newlywed and recent college grad. She and her husband decided to track spending

Multiple Bank Accounts

Some people track spending by using different bank accounts. For example, they could put some income into a savings account. They use one checking account for fixed expenses. Another checking account is for variable expenses. This makes it easier to see how much money is available.

in two categories. But they struggled with budgeting apps. The apps were slow to update new transactions in their accounts. They wanted something more immediate. McCallson said,

> *I created a spreadsheet we keep on our phones. Every time we spend money in those categories, we write it on the spreadsheet. Then we subtract it from the total. That way we always know how much money we have left. Writing it down also keeps us aware of our spending.*[4]

REVIEWING SPENDING

People also need to set a time to review their spending. For many people, setting a weekly review time works well. People

Keeping track of planned and actual expenses can help a person adjust a budget as needed.

compare the past week's spending with the budget plan. If they spent too much in a category, they plan to spend less the next week. This is also a good time to celebrate progress made toward financial goals.

Reviewing a budget will also show if it needs adjusting. A person could spend less than expected in a category. He could reduce his budget to match. This would free up money for other goals. A person might find he is often spending too much in a category. He may need to increase the budget for that category.

CHANGING MONEY HABITS

It is important to identify harmful financial habits. For example, some people spend money when they are stressed or bored. Kristy Archuleta is a professor in financial planning. She says, "Maybe when you're stressed, you know you're going to spend more money because that's how you cope with that stress. So maybe you get up and go for a walk instead of sitting at your computer looking through Amazon."[5]

Too much **impulse spending** is another harmful habit. People are surrounded by advertising that encourages impulse spending. To fight this, experts say it can help to wait 24 hours before making purchases. For larger purchases, it can help to wait several days. This gives the emotional part of the brain a chance to calm down. It also gives people time to think of the pros and cons. After waiting a few days, a person might decide the purchase isn't worth the money.

Taking time to think over a big purchase, such as a new TV, can help prevent buyer's remorse.

Spending too much time on social media can lead people to make expensive or impulsive purchases.

Social media can also drive harmful spending. Research shows a growing trend of people making unaffordable purchases after seeing them online. Camilla Ericson struggled with this. She says,

> *I was buying too many products I saw on social media. Influencers make them look unrealistically amazing. Sometimes I need to limit my time on Instagram so I stay on my budget better.*[6]

Tracking and reviewing is an important way to stay aware of spending habits. It helps people tackle problems before they get too big. It also helps people see their successes. It can keep a budget on track.

LIVING LIFE ON A BUDGET

Taylor Phillip is known as Taylor Budgets on social media. She shares her budgeting journey online. She tells people how she got out of debt on her small income. Phillip says, "You must adopt a mindset of financial literacy. It is much easier to manage your money than get caught up in a cycle of overspending, debt payments, and horrible decision making."[7]

Learning how to budget is an important life skill.

Living on a budget does require choices. However, this also has benefits. Kevin Ericson is a newlywed on a tight budget. He says, "Budgeting is fun because it makes me realize what I truly love in life. It forces me to choose what is most important."[8]

REMEMBERING GOALS

Life has many ups and downs. Sometimes unexpected expenses come up. People might see friends having expensive fun on social media. Or they might get tired of tracking and reviewing their budget. Sometimes people make spending mistakes. They might want to give up. Reminding themselves why they budget can help people stick with it.

Some people keep reminders of their goals and values where they see them often. For example, a person could put a picture of a car on her mirror. She could put a note next to it saying: *I am saving $500 each month toward my car. Twenty-two more months to go.* Another note might say: *I am saving for an emergency fund. I do not want to panic during every hard time.*

All-or-Nothing Thinking

It can be tempting to give up on a budget after unexpected expenses or spending mistakes. People might think their monthly budget is ruined. They may give up and decide to start over next month. This is called all-or-nothing thinking. But progress is more important than perfection for financial goals. An imperfect budget is better than not having one at all.

Budgets are not about cutting out all fun.

She might also put some savings toward paying down her credit card. That note could read: *I am paying off my credit card debt. My money should go toward my favorite charity instead of interest payments*.

Odin Crooks has a different way to stay motivated. After finishing high school, he got an **apprenticeship**. He studied to become a heating, ventilation, and air conditioning technician. He said, "When I want to overspend, I remind myself how many hours of work it will cost me. I also remind myself that I'm saving money to buy tools for my job."[9]

KEEPING LIFE FUN

Living on a budget does not mean people can't have fun. Phillip says,

I feel like there's a ***stigma*** *around budgeting, that it is restricting and that you have to cancel out all of your wants. But that is not true. . . . I'm going to continue to love Starbucks, so instead of canceling it out of my budget, I incorporate it into my budget.*[10]

Some people also motivate themselves by putting leftover money into their "fun money." This rewards them for reducing costs.

Many people find it easier to keep their budget if they have an accountability partner. Accountability partners can celebrate each other's financial successes. They can also brainstorm creative solutions to budget problems.

Living on a budget takes practice and consistency. But budgeting is an important financial skill. It can help people meet their goals. It can help people live in a sustainable and enjoyable way. It can lead to financial freedom and peace of mind.

Learning to budget sets people up for financial success.

GLOSSARY

apprenticeship

a program where a person learns a skill or trade

impulse spending

when a person makes a sudden unplanned purchase without thinking it through

insufficient

not enough

net

a person's income after taxes, insurance, and other deductions are taken out

overdraft fee

a fee charged when an account lacks enough money to cover all transactions

spreadsheet

an electronic document that uses rows and columns to arrange and calculate data

statements

documents that report all the activity in an account

stigma

a negative attitude about an idea or person

SOURCE NOTES

CHAPTER ONE: CREATING A BUDGET

1. Quoted in Mogaland, "Unlock Your Financial Freedom," *Medium*, July 18, 2023. http://medium.com.

CHAPTER TWO: BALANCING A BUDGET

2. Miriam Johnson, Personal interview, October 19, 2023.

3. William Johnson, Personal interview, October 18, 2023.

CHAPTER THREE: STICKING TO A BUDGET

4. Megan McCallson, Personal interview, October 14, 2023.

5. Quoted in Leigh Beeson, "How You Think About Money Affects What You Do with It," *University of Georgia*, March 15, 2022. http://news.uga.edu.

6. Camilla Ericson, Personal interview, November 23, 2023.

CHAPTER FOUR: LIVING LIFE ON A BUDGET

7. Taylor Phillip, "The Budgeting Mindset with Taylor Budgets," *YouTube*, uploaded by onomy, March 21, 2023. www.youtube.com.

8. Kevin Ericson, Personal interview, November 23, 2023.

9. Odin Crooks, Personal interview, October 20, 2023.

10. Taylor Phillip, "Budgeting for Beginners | A Low-Income Detailed Budget with Me," *YouTube*, uploaded by TaylorBudgets, August 8, 2022. www.youtube.com.

FOR FURTHER RESEARCH

BOOKS

Jean Chatzky, Kathryn Tuggle, and the HerMoney Team, *How to Money: Your Ultimate Visual Guide to the Basics of Finance*. New York: Roaring Brook, 2022.

Emma Huddleston, *Living on a Budget*. San Diego, CA: BrightPoint Press, 2020.

Ruth Owen, *Budgeting*. Minneapolis, MN: Bearport, 2023.

INTERNET SOURCES

"How to Make Passive Income as a Teenager: 5 Ideas," *Greenlight*, n.d., http://greenlight.com.

Bev O'Shea and Lauren Schwahn, "Budgeting 101: How to Budget Money," *NerdWallet*, July 28, 2023. www.nerdwallet.com.

"Teen Banking: Budgeting for Teens," *Copper*, n.d., www.getcopper.com.

WEBSITES

How Money Smart Are You?
http://playmoneysmart.fdic.gov

The FDIC is a government agency that oversees financial institutions. This suite of resources includes fourteen games to help educate people on various financial skills.

NerdWallet
www.nerdwallet.com

NerdWallet is a personal finance company that has articles on many topics, including budgets.

Experian
www.experian.com

Experian is a consumer credit reporting company that has many budgeting articles.

INDEX

IMAGE CREDITS

Cover: © Nikita Wayhome/Shutterstock Images
5: © everydayplus/Shutterstock Images
7: © fizkes/Shutterstock Images
8: © digitalskillet/Shutterstock Images
11: © Nikita Wayhome/Shutterstock Images
12: © Quality Stock Arts/Shutterstock Images
15: © Foolish Productions/Shutterstock Images
17: © Jason Cox/Shutterstock Images
18: © Piece of Cake/Shutterstock Images
21: © Natee Meepian/Shutterstock Images
24: © Red Line Editorial
27: © Prostock-Studio/Shutterstock Images
29: © DGLImages/Shutterstock Images
31: © mooremedia/Shutterstock Images
32: © Gulpa/Shutterstock Images
36: © Dmytro Zinkevych/Shutterstock Images
39: © Andrii Iemelianenko/Shutterstock Images
40: © Kmpzzz/Shutterstock Images
44: © Ryan R. Fox/Shutterstock Images
47: © Andrey_Popov/Shutterstock Images
48: © Egoitz Bengoetxea/Shutterstock Images
51: © BearFotos/Shutterstock Images
54: © Ground Picture/Shutterstock Images
57: © Wongsakorn Napaeng/Shutterstock Images

ABOUT THE AUTHOR

Jenny Crooks-Johnson is an author who writes fiction and nonfiction books for children. She lives in Colorado with her amazing family. She would like to dedicate this book to her mom, Rita Crooks, who could make a dollar go further than anyone else. Her mom also taught her that life can be full, even when bank accounts aren't. She'd also like to dedicate it to all her young-adult children and nieces and nephews who let her interview them for this book. Keep making the best financial decisions you can!